£7.99

Welcome

SCOOBY-DOO!
Annual 2012

J2211 024
£9.75

Scooby Story!

Scooby Story!

Scooby Story!

Scooby Story!

He's Scooby-
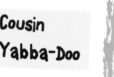
Dooper!

Find out all about Scooby-Doo with these fun and silly facts!

Family Doo!

Scooby-Doo comes from a really big family of pooches, here are some of his closest relations...

Daddy-Doo

Mommy-Doo

Cousin Yabba-Doo

Sister Roobie-Doo

Top Travels!

Check out some of Scooby's favourite holiday snaps! Can you work out which country each photo was taken in?

Scooby made some new pals down under!
Answer:

Checking out the home of pizza!
Answer:

Looking for leprechauns!
Answer:

Favourite Things!

Favourite colour: Brown

Favourite food:

SCOOBY SNACKS

Favourite sport: Football

MOMMY-DOO'S BIG BOOK OF YUMMY RECIPES

Favourite book:

Favourite holiday: Christmas

Worst Things!

Monsters

Running out of snacks

Smelly socks

Getting up in the morning

Cats (Scooby is scared of them)

⑤

THE CREEPING HORROR

Sigh

SHAGGY, WHAT'S TAKING YOU AND SCOOBY SO LONG WITH THAT SPARE TIRE?

JOHN ROZUM - script
DON PERLIN - pencils
SCOTT McREA - inks
JOHN COSTANZA - letters
PAUL BECTON - colors
HARVEY RICHARDS - assists
HEIDI MacDONALD - edits

LIKE, WE NEED A SPARE TIRE FOR THE SPARE TIRE.

I GUESS WE FORGOT TO GET IT FIXED AFTER THE LAST TIME WE HAD A FLAT TIRE.

WHAT I WANT TO KNOW IS, LIKE, WHY WE ALWAYS BREAK DOWN ON CREEPY OLD ROADS INSTEAD OF THE HIGHWAY, OR AT THE MALL?

REAH, REEPY!

IT LOOKS LIKE WE'RE NOT THE FIRST CAR TO BREAK DOWN ALONG THIS ROAD.

EDALV

LOOK, THERE'S A LIGHT OVER THERE. MAYBE THEY'LL LET US USE THEIR PHONE.

LET'S GO FIND OUT.

WOW! THINGAMAJIG TECHNOLOGIES. THEY MAKE SOFT-SERVE ICE CREAM DISPENSERS.

AND COMPUTERS, SATELLITES, FIRE SAFETY EQUIPMENT, SUBMARINES-- PRETTY MUCH EVERY-THING.

THINGAMAJIG TECHNOLOGIES INC.

THAT'S ODD. NO ONE SEEMS TO BE AROUND. I WONDER WHERE THE GUARD IS?

SOMEONE'S HERE. MAYBE THEY CAN GIVE US SOME ANSWERS.

ENTRANCE

BZZZ

YES, CAN I HELP YOU? MY NAME IS DR. SLAVINSKI.

SORRY TO BOTHER YOU, BUT OUR VAN BROKE DOWN JUST UP THE ROAD, AND WE WANTED TO KNOW IF WE COULD US A PHONE TO CALL A TOW TRUCK.

ALL RIGHT, BUT PLEASE HURRY. I'VE GOT A LOT OF WORK TO DO HERE.

ENTR

WHERE'S EVERYONE ELSE?

YOU HAVEN'T HEARD?

OVER THE PAST WEEK, THE SCIENTISTS WORKING HERE HAVE BEEN TERRORIZED BY SOME SORT OF CREEPING HORROR.

PROFESSOR ALVA SAID IT IS ONE OF THE EXPERIMENTS GONE HAYWIRE, BUT ONLY ONE THING IS KNOWN FOR SURE-- THREE DAYS AGO, EVERYONE FLED THE BUILDING.

NOBODY HAS BEEN BACK SINCE-- EXCEPT ME.

IF THIS CREATURE IS SO HORRIBLE, THEN WHY DID YOU COME BACK?

MY WORK IS TOO IMPORTANT. BESIDES, I'M HOPING TO FIGURE OUT A WAY TO CAPTURE THE CREATURE FOR STUDY.

HOW WERE YOU PLANNING ON CAPTURING THIS CREEPING HORROR, DR. SLAVINSKI?

THAT'S TOP SECRET.

MAYBE WE CAN HELP. WE HAVE A LOT OF EXPERIENCE SOLVING MYSTERIES, ESPECIALLY ONES INVOLVING MONSTERS.

FINE. JUST DON'T TOUCH ANYTHING. THIS EQUIPMENT IS ONE OF A KIND AND VERY EXPENSIVE.

RHAT AROUT THE ROW TRUCK?

GRRRRRRR!

THE TOW TRUCK WILL HAVE TO WAIT UNTIL WE SOLVE THIS MYSTERY, SCOOBY.

LET'S SPLIT UP AND LOOK FOR CLUES!

BOY, WE SURE LUCKED OUT, SCOOBY. ALL THESE JARS HAVE COMPLETE SERVINGS OF FOOD IN EACH PILL. THIS ONE IS ICE CREAM!

MMM. JUST LIKE THE REAL THING. I'VE GOT TO ASK MY DOCTOR FOR A PRESCRIPTION.

PISTACHIO ICE CREAM PILLS

RICKEN RALAD RANDWICH!

HERE, TRY THE TUNA ON WHOLE WHEAT. COULD YOU PLEASE PASS THE POTATO SALAD?

RAVE ROME ROMATO ROUP.

THANK YOU, I DON'T MIND IF I DO!

ROW, TO ROSH IT ROWN RITH SROME RATER.

GOOD IDEA. I WONDER WHAT THESE ARE?

WARNING ADD WATER TO PILLS BEFORE SWALLOWING

UH-OH.

SCOOBY, WAIT! DON'T DRINK THAT...

...WATER.

GLU, GUL?

FOSOONT!

PLOOI

I GUESS I SHOULD HAVE READ THE LABELS BETTER, MYSELF. SORRY, SCOOB.

I GUESS WE'LL HAVE TO ROLL YOU AROUND UNTIL YOU GO BACK TO NORMAL.

LFWOOP!

THAT'S STRANGE.

WHAT IS IT, VELMA?

IT LOOKS LIKE A PIECE OF SHAG CARPET. BUT, THERE ISN'T ANY CARPET IN THIS WHOLE BUILDING.

JEEPERS! THAT'S NOT A PIECE OF CARPET, IT'S A PIECE OF *THAT!*

THE CREEPING HORROR!

RUN!

QUICK! IN HERE!

CLOSE THE DOOR!

I'M PRETTY SURE THAT THING CAN'T OPEN DOORS.

I SURE HOPE YOU'RE RIGHT.

I'M BETTING THAT THING CAN'T PRY OPEN FILING CABINETS EITHER.

ALL THESE NUMBERED DISCS CONTAIN RESEARCH DATA. SOME OF THEM ARE MISSING.

WHAT WOULD A CREATURE LIKE THAT WANT WITH SOMEBODY'S RESEARCH FILES?

MAYBE DR. SLAVINSKI CAN ANSWER THAT.

STORY CONTINUES ON PAGE 12

WHY, IT WAS NOTHING MORE THAN A TOY REMOTE-CONTROL CAR COVERED WITH GARBAGE BAGS, PLASTIC BUBBLE WRAP, AND AN OLD ORANGE SHAG CARPET!

AND THAT MYSTERIOUS CLOAKED FIGURE WAS CONTROLLING IT WITH THAT REMOTE CONTROL!

HE'S GETTING AWAY! SHAGGY, YOU'VE GOT TO STOP HIM!

SHRAGGY, RO!

DID YOU SAY "ROLL," SCOOBY?

RO! RO! RO!

ROLLLLLL

BONK!

YES! STEE-RIKE!

GROOVY GAMES!

Point the finger!

Velma is busy doing some detective work with these finger prints! Can you help her to match each one with it's matching pair?

1
2
3
4
5
6

A
B
C
D
E
F

ICE SCREAM!

Shaggy is buying an ice cream but that mean old Cotton Candy Monster has mixed up all the flavours! Help Shaggy to unscramble each flavour.

A LCTOCEOAH

B NBANAA

C NGMOA

D CKOEOIS NDA MCREA

E ALVNAIL

F UTTTI RTFIIU

GRID LOCKED!

Give Fred a hand rounding up these villains and fitting them into the grid. Use the letters already in the grid to help you fit them in.

ALIEN (5)
HAG (3)   GHOST (5)
WITCH (5)   BIG FOOT (3, 4)
MONSTER (7)
GREMLIN (7)
VAMPIRE (7)

When is it bad luck to meet a black cat?

When you're a mouse!

Why was there a fence around the graveyard? Because people were dying to get in!

AUSTRALIA-- THE LAND DOWN UNDER!

A COUNTRY WITH UNUSUAL *WILDLIFE* AND AN EXTREMELY DELICATE *ECOSYSTEM* THAT MUST BE PROTECTED!

HERRIOT *WILDLIFE* PRESERVE

POACHING STRICTLY PROHIBITED

QUIET NIGHT, EH, JED?

NOT ALL *THAT* QUIET, MATE! GOT SOME WONKY NOISES OVER IN *SECTOR-7.* CHECK IT OUT!

WONKY NOISES, HE SAYS! IT'S A *WILDLIFE RESERVE*-- IT'S *FILLED* WITH WONKY NOISES!

RUSSLE RUSSLE

SCRAPE

HMM. THEN AGAIN, COULD BE *POACHERS!*

OI! YOU IN THE *BUSH!* LET'S HAVE A LOOK AT YOUR *SECURITY PASS,* EH?

SCOOBY-DOO 81. April, 2004. Published monthly by DC Comics, 1700 Broadway, New York, NY 10019. POSTMASTER: Send address changes to SCOOBY-DOO, DC Comics Subscriptions, P.O. Box 0528, Baldwin, NY 11510. Annual subscription rate (12 issues) $27.00. Canadian subscribers must add $12.00 for postage and GST. GST # is R125921072. All foreign countries must add $12.00 for postage. U.S. funds only. Copyright © 2004 Hanna-Barbera. All Rights Reserved. SCOOBY-DOO and all related characters and elements are trademarks of and © Hanna-Barbera. The stories, characters and incidents mentioned in this magazine are entirely fictional. Printed on recyclable paper. DC Comics does not read or accept unsolicited submissions of ideas, stories or artwork.
Printed in Canada.

DC Comics, a Warner Bros. Entertainment Company

• DAN DIDIO, VP-Editorial • PAUL LEVITZ, President & Publisher • GEORG BREWER, VP-Design & Retail Product Development •
• RICHARD BRUNING, Senior. VP-Creative Director • PATRICK CALDON, Senior VP-Finance & Operations • CHRIS CARAMALIS, VP-Finance • TERRI CUNNINGHAM, VP-Managing Editor •
• ALISON GILL, VP-Manufacturing • LILLIAN LASERSON, Senior. VP & General Counsel • JIM LEE, Editorial Director-Wildstorm •
• DAVID McKILLIPS, VP-Advertising Custom Publishing • JOHN NEE, VP-Business Development • Gregory Noveck, Senior VP-Creative Affairs •
• CHERYL RUBIN, VP-Brand Management • BOB WAYNE, VP-Sales & Marketing •

OUR **SECURITY** IS EXTREMELY TIGHT. IT'S **DESIGNED** TO KEEP OUTSIDE ANIMALS AWAY!

SOUNDS LIKE YOU'RE **AFRAID** OF SOMETHING!

THAT'S RIGHT-- **HOUSE CATS**.

HOUSE CATS? ARE YOU SERIOUS?

COMPLETELY. CATS AREN'T **NATIVE** TO THIS COUNTRY. AT SOME POINT, THEY WERE BROUGHT IN ILLEGALLY AND HAVE BRED IN STAGGERING NUMBERS.

THESE CATS RUN WILD ALL OVER AUSTRALIA, HAVING REGRESSED TO A **FERAL** STATE. THEY'RE A MAJOR **THREAT** TO OUR NATIVE WILDLIFE, AND THAT'S THE VERY REASON WE'VE ESTABLISHED THIS RESERVE-- TO **PROTECT** AUSTRALIA'S ANIMALS!

GETTING BACK TO OUR MYSTERY... ARE THERE ANY **SUSPECTS?** ANY **BUSINESS RIVALS,** MAYBE?

I'M AFRAID NOT. WE'RE **GOVERNMENT-SANCTIONED** AND OWN THE LAND OUTRIGHT. WE BOUGHT THE PROPERTY **YEARS** AGO FROM **FARNHAM INDUSTRIAL.**

THAT'S GOTTA BE IT-- FARNHAM'S INVOLVED!

NO, I THINK IT HAS TO BE **POACHERS,** DAPHNE. THEY'RE THE ONLY PEOPLE WHO'D **PROFIT** FROM THIS SCAM!

GUYS? AREN'T YOU **FORGETTING** SOMETHING? WHAT IF THERE'S --GULP-- A **REAL** SABERTOOTH TIGER?

SHAGGY, AREN'T **YOU** FORGETTING SOMETHING? THE SABERTOOTH TIGER IS **EXTINCT!**

BAH! THERE IS NO *CONCLUSIVE PROOF* THE SABERTOOTH IS EXTINCT!

WHA--?!? WHO ARE *YOU?*

NORBERT BURKE, NATURALIST AND EXPERT TRACKER, AT YOUR SERVICE!

BELIEVE YOU ME, MATES, I'VE TRACKED DOWN MORE ELUSIVE BEASTIES THAN YOU CAN SHAKE A STICK AT! SO WHO'S GONNA *HELP* ME SNIFF OUT THIS SABERTOOTH, EH?

SORRY-- WE'VE GOT TO INVESTIGATE *FARNHAM INDUSTRIAL!*

AND I WANT THIS GUARD TO HELP ME CHECK THE *SECURITY SYSTEM!*

THAT'S THE SPIRIT! GOOD OF YOU TO *VOLUNTEER,* BOYS!

WHO... *US?!?*

RUH?

I FOUND THE TIGER HIDING IN THE BUSH, BUT ISN'T IT POSSIBLE HE'S HOLED UP IN ONE OF THOSE *CAVES?*

LET'S CHECK ON THE *SECURITY FENCES* FIRST.

I HAVE A HUNCH OUR *SABERTOOTH* WAS BROUGHT IN FROM *OUTSIDE.* WHEN I GET A HUNCH, I'M ALMOST *ALWAYS* RIGHT...

REALLY?

WELL, NOT *ALWAYS*. BUT THIS TIME, I'M *POSITIVE!*

MEANWHILE...

COME IN! WHAT CAN I DO FOR YOU LADIES?

FARNHAM INDUSTRIAL

WELL, MR. FARNHAM, IT SEEMS THE *HERRIOT RESERVE* IS BEING TERRORIZED BY AN UNKNOWN ASSAILANT. SOMEONE TRYING TO ACQUIRE THEIR *LAND* FOR THEMSELVES, PERHAPS--!

YOU WOULDN'T KNOW ANYTHING ABOUT IT, WOULD YOU?

TAKE A GANDER AT MY *COMPLEX*, LADIES. IMPRESSIVE, ISN'T IT? I WOULDN'T *HAVE* IT IF NOT FOR *HERRIOT!* I MADE A *FORTUNE* SELLING HIM THAT LAND. WHY WOULD I WANT TO HURT THE MAN?

HMM. THAT *IS* A GOOD POINT--

HERE'S ANOTHER GOOD POINT-- I'M *PRO-ENVIRONMENT*. I EVEN OWN MY OWN *ZOO*. HERRIOT'S DOING IMPORTANT WORK, AND I TOTALLY SUPPORT HIM!

IF YOU THINK *I'M* A SUSPECT, THEN YOU'RE ON THE *WRONG TRAIL!*

WE'RE ON THE *RIGHT* TRAIL FOR SURE, MATES! LOOK-- *TIGER TRACKS!* LITTLE DEVIL *IS* PROBABLY HIDING IN ONE OF THE CAVES!

THEN WHY DOES THE TRAIL LEAD OVER *THERE?*

STORY CONTINUES ON PAGE 28

25

How to Draw SCOOBY-DOO!

FOLLOW THESE SIMPLE STEPS TO CREATE YOUR OWN DRAWINGS OF THAT LOVEABLE SCAREDY-DOG, SCOOBY-DOO!!

1

Follow the steps from 1 - 4 to draw Scooby-Doo. Can you see how it starts with a circle and an egg shape to create his body? Follow the steps as closely as you can and use a pencil so you can rub out any unwanted lines as you go.

2

Carefully copy the lines to add shape to his head and body.

3

Now complete his legs and paws and add his dog tag.

4

Use a pen to draw in your final shape. Add the details - his ears, expression and the marks on his coat. Finally, rub out any unwanted pencil lines. This should leave you with a fantastic Scooby sketch!

These three steps will help you to draw a Scooby portrait. Start with a sausage shape for his head and neck. Add a large oval for his nose and build on it from there. When you get to the last step, use a pen to draw your final sketch and rub out any unwanted lines.

1

2

3

Now have a go for yourself! Follow the steps to create your own Scooby scene below.

-:WHEW!:- BOY, THAT WAS CLOSE! BUT AT LEAST WE'RE **SAFE** OUT HERE!

UH... RRRAGGY--?

DON'T SWEAT IT, SCOOB. IT'S JUST, LIKE, A FEW LITTLE **CATS**--!

HISSS

HELP!!!

CLAW

MRRAOW

SCRATCH

DANG IT ALL! SABERTOOTH RAN OFF! WHAT THE DEVIL HAPPENED TO **YOU** TWO?

RITTIES!

K-KITTIES! **LOTS** AND **LOTS** OF KITTIES!

AND YOUR FINDINGS...?

WE STILL BELIEVE **FARNHAM** IS RESPONSIBLE, EVEN THOUGH WE DON'T HAVE **PROOF**!

AND I STILL SAY IT'S A **SECURITY BREACH**, EVEN THOUGH I HAVE NO PROOF!

WE'VE GOT YOUR PROOF, FRED! THERE'S A **HOLE** IN THE FENCE-- WE'VE SEEN IT!

HA! I WAS RIGHT!

NO, YOU WERE **WRONG.** YA SEE, THERE ACTUALLY **IS** A SABERTOOTH ON THE LOOSE!

NOT TO MENTION PUSSYCATS. THEY'RE **WORSE** THAN THE TIGER!

TEETH LIKE *KNIVES!* CLAWS LIKE *DAGGERS!* HE'S BIG AS LIFE!

A REAL SABERTOOTH? WELL, *THIS* PUTS AN UNEXPECTED TWIST ON THINGS!

DR. HERRIOT, DOES YOUR INSTITUTE HAVE ACCESS TO *FEDERAL ANIMAL REGISTRY* RECORDS?

EH? YES, OF COURSE.

FILE STORAGE
AUTHORIZED PERSONNEL ONLY

WE'RE CLOSELY ASSOCIATED WITH THE REGISTRY, AND SHARE INFORMATION WITH THEM.

ALL ON *COMPUTER*, OF COURSE. I'LL PUT IN MY ACCESS CODE AND YOU CAN HAVE A LOOK.

WHAT'S UP, VELMA?

JUST A *HUNCH*, DAPHNE.

VELMA, ISN'T THIS KIND OF A WASTE OF TIME? I MEAN, IF THE TIGER IS *REAL*--

THAT'S EXACTLY WHAT I'M LOOKING FOR-- A *REAL TIGER!*

GENTLEMEN, NOW THAT WE KNOW WHAT WE'RE DEALING WITH, WHAT SHOULD WE *DO?*

ONLY ONE THING *TO* DO, DOCTOR--

--A TIGER HUNT!

C'MON, SCOOBY-- THAT'S OUR CUE TO LEAVE!

NOT SO FAST!

NO! LIKE, WE'RE NOT VOLUNTEERING AND YOU CAN'T MAKE US!!! CAN YOU?

HEY, WHAT ABOUT THAT IDEA OF YOURS-- THAT THE TIGER LIVES IN THE CAVES?

THIS TIME I'VE GOT A FEELING WE'LL FIND HIM WHERE WE DID BEFORE. THE CRIMINAL ALWAYS RETURNS TO THE SCENE OF THE CRIME, EH?

DO YOU REALLY THINK A TIGER TRAP WILL WORK?

LIKE A CHARM, MATE! BUT WE'LL NEED SOME BAIT TO LURE 'IM WITH. GOT SOMETHING SPECIAL IN THE BACK.

I'LL GET IT!

WONDER WHAT KIND OF BAIT WORKS ON SABERTOOTH TIGERS--?

LIKE, WOWZERS! A GOURMET ROAST! SEEMS TOO GOOD TO WASTE ON AN OL' TIGER, WOULDN'T YOU SAY, OL' PAL?

MMM! RRREAH!

MM-MMM! JUST A LITTLE *SAMPLE.* I'M SURE THAT OVERGROWN TOMCAT WON'T KNOW THE DIFFERENCE.

ULP! D-D-DID YOU SAY SOMETHING, SCOOBY?

RRRUH-UH!

LIKE, I WAS AFRAID YOU'D SAY THAT--!

YOIKS!! WHAT A SOREHEAD!

WOW! SHAGGY, *QUICK--JUMP THROUGH* THE *HOLE* IN THE FENCE!

IT'S NOT OUR FAULT! WE ONLY WANTED A *TASTE!!!*

LIKE, WHY'D FRED TELL US TO GO THROUGH THE *FENCE?* AND WHY'D I *LISTEN?*

THAT'S JUST IT. I CHECKED THE **RECORDS** ON FARNHAM'S ZOO, AND HE HAPPENS TO OWN A TIGER THAT TURNS OUT TO BE OUR **SABERTOOTH.** FARNHAM PUT **FAKE FANGS** ON HIM!

BUT **WHY** WOULD HE PULL THIS CON ON HERRIOT?

THE **ANSWER** WAS IN ONE OF THE **CAVES.** SEE?

LOOKS LIKE...**ANCIENT FOSSILS?**

EXACTLY! PERFECTLY PRESERVED PREHISTORIC FOSSILS AND ARTIFACTS!

THEY'RE WORTH A HUGE **FORTUNE,** BUT FARNHAM NO LONGER OWNS THIS PROPERTY. HE PLANNED TO GET IT BACK BY **SCARING** HERRIOT, THEN SELLING THE LAND TO AN **ARCHAEOLOGICAL FOUNDATION!**

AND I WOULD'VE GOT AWAY WITH IT, TOO, IF NOT FOR YOU **MEDDLING KIDS--!**

THERE'S A GOOD TIGER! WE'LL RID THESE NASTY FANGS FOR YOU--!

PRETTY **SMART,** VELMA, BUT LET'S NOT FORGET **SHAGGY** AND **SCOOBY-DOO--** THEY WERE AWFULLY **BRAVE** HANDLING THE TIGER!

AW, SHUCKS. THE **REAL** HEROES ARE THOSE LITTLE **CATS!**

YOU'RE RIGHT, SHAGGY! DON'T YOU THINK THEY DESERVE A **REWARD?**

SURE! BUT DO **WE** HAVE TO GIVE IT TO THEM--?

PURRRR....!

BRRR!

END

33

Scary Shadows!

1 **2** **3** **4** **5** **6** **7** **8**

A **B** **C** **D** **E** **F** **G** **H**

Poor Shaggy is spooked by all the scary shadows in this haunted house! Can you match each shadow up with the object it belongs to?

Write your answers here:

1
2
3
4
5
6
7
8

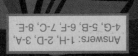

Answers: 1-H, 2-D, 3-A, 4-G, 5-B, 6-F, 7-C, 8-E.

DIG THEM BONES

-- "BREAD OF THE DEAD."

ZOINKS! I THINK I'LL PASS!

RHEE TOO.

JOHN ROZUM - WRITER
JOE STATON - PENCILLER
DAVE HUNT - INKER
RYAN CLINE - LETTERER

PAUL BECTON - COLORS
HARVEY RICHARDS - ASST EDITOR
JOAN HILTY - EDITOR

SHAGGY, YOU AND SCOOBY ARE THE BIGGEST COWARDS IN THE WORLD!

AND I WANT YOU TO KNOW THAT WE'RE VERY PROUD OF THAT RECORD, AND WE PLAN TO KEEP IT UP!

WE BROUGHT YOU TWO CHICKENS HERE TO SHOW YOU THAT SKELETONS AREN'T ALWAYS SOMETHING THAT YOU NEED TO FEAR.

DAPHNE'S RIGHT. THE MEXICAN DAY OF THE DEAD HOLIDAY IS A TIME TO *CELEBRATE* THE MEMORY OF FRIENDS AND FAMILY WHO ARE NO LONGER LIVING.

IT'S ALSO A CELEBRATION OF THE CYCLE OF LIFE.

IT'S A HAPPY TIME MEANT FOR REJOICING, NOT MOURNING.

LIKE, CHECK IT OUT, SCOOBY. ALL THE MERCHANTS ARE GIVING THE GHOULS IN THE COFFINS FREE ORANGES.

HEE HEE. GOOD ONE, SCOOB!

RUCKY STIFFS.

PLEASE, HELP YOURSELVES!

YOU GUYS WERE RIGHT, NOT ALL SKELETONS ARE SCARY!

SCOOB AND I LIKE THESE CREEPY SKELETONS, RIGHT, SCOOB?

REAH! REAH!

ROO CAN REAT THEM!

THAT'S RIGHT, SCOOB, AND ANYTHING YOU CAN EAT IS OKAY BY US.

NOW, WHICH ONE TO--

N-N-N-NO PROBLEM, WE'LL BE OUT OF YOUR HAIR--

UH... ⌐HEH HEH⌐ ...OR WHATEVER YOU SKELETONS WEAR UNDER YOUR SOMBREROS-- RIGHT AWAY...

JUST LET ME GET SOME CANDY FOR THE...

...ROAD?

HMPH!

LEAVE NOW--

-- OR NEVER LEAVE AGAIN!

IF OUR ILLUSTRIOUS ANCESTOR WANTS YOU TO LEAVE, THEN YOU MUST GO!

WE CANNOT LET OUTSIDERS BRING ILL FORTUNE TO OUR TOWN!

YOU HEARD THEM, LET'S GET OUT OF HERE!

RUN!

39

JINKIES! I CAN'T BELIEVE WE CAME ALL THIS WAY ONLY TO HAVE TO TURN BACK SO SOON.

LIKE, I HATE TO TELL YOU, FREDDIE, BUT THIS VAN ISN'T AN OFF-ROAD VEHICLE.

FRED, WHY ARE YOU STOPPING? ALL THE OTHER TOURISTS ARE GOING TO LEAVE US BEHIND.

I'M COUNTING ON THAT. SOMETHING SMELLS FISHY AROUND HERE.

DON'T LOOK AT ME OR SCOOB. WE HAVEN'T EATEN FISH IN DAYS!

I THINK WHAT FREDDIE'S TRYING TO SAY IS THAT THERE'S A MYSTERY HERE THAT NEEDS SOLVING.

THAT'S RIGHT, VELMA. LET'S HEAD BACK TO THE TOWN AND SEE IF WE CAN FIND SOME CLUES.

LIKE, I DON'T KNOW MUCH ABOUT CUSTOMS HERE, GANG, BUT THAT CRAZY SKELETON WAS PRETTY CLEAR WHEN HE TOLD US TO LEAVE.

AND I'D HATE TO BE SEEN AS RUDE!

RHEE EITHER.

BELCH

NOW TO SEE WHO THIS FOUNDING FATHER REALLY IS.

¡SEÑOR SANCHEZ! BUT WHY?

I WORRY THAT TOO MANY TOURISTS WILL COMMERCIALIZE OUR EL DIA DE LOS MUERTOS FESTIVAL, AND THAT OUR CUSTOMS WILL DISAPPEAR AS THEY HAVE IN MANY OTHER PLACES.

I CAN UNDERSTAND THAT. BUT IT'S YOUR CUSTOMS THAT BROUGHT US HERE TO YOUR TOWN. WE WANTED TO EXPERIENCE THEM FIRST-HAND.

TOMORROW IS THE DAY WE SPEND DECORATING THE CEMETERY. AFTERWARDS, THERE IS A BIG PICNIC. WILL YOU PLEASE JOIN US?

WE'D BE HAPPY TO.

WELL, NOW WE'LL PROBABLY NEVER GET SHAGGY AND SCOOBY OVER THEIR FEAR OF SKELETONS.

YEAH, ABOUT THE ONLY THING THAT PAIR HAS IN COMMON WITH A SKELETON IS THAT NONE OF THEM HAS ANY GUTS.

I WOULDN'T WORRY ABOUT THAT...

OH, IF ONLY ALL THE SKELETONS WE FACED WERE SO DELICIOUS!

I REALLY RIG RESE RONES.

I DIG 'EM TOO, SCOOB.

MUNCH

CHEW

CHOMP

MUNCH

HA HA HA HA HA HA HA

THE END

SAVE THE WORLD!

Do your bit to save the planet with these Scoob-tastic recycling bins! All you need to do is make your recycling bin, put it on a shelf and start saving your paper, plastic and cans.

YOU WILL NEED:
thick card,
2 cardboard boxes,
scissors, PVA glue,
newspaper, a plate,
paints and
a paintbrush

PAPER

CANS

1

Draw the shape of Shaggy onto a large piece of thick card and cut him out.

2

Place a plate onto Shaggy's tummy and draw around it. Cut out the circle that you have drawn.

3

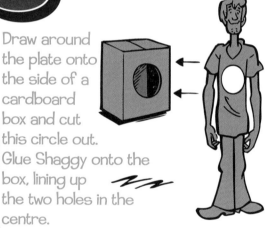

Draw around the plate onto the side of a cardboard box and cut this circle out. Glue Shaggy onto the box, lining up the two holes in the centre.

4

Cover the whole thing with 2-3 layers of PVA glue and torn up newspaper and leave it to dry.

5

Paint Shaggy with black, green, brown and orange paints. Decide what you would like to recycle and use chunky letters to spell it out on Shaggy's t-shirt. Paint over the letters with black paint. Paint the sides of the box too.

6

Place the box on a shelf, so that Shaggy's legs hang over the side. Now you are ready to start recycling! You can make a Scooby version too, just follow the same steps but draw a Scooby shape in step 1.

NORMALLY, WE DON'T ALLOW DOGS...IF THERE IS ANY DAMAGE WE *WILL* HOLD YOU RESPONSIBLE...

ALL RIGHT, THANK YOU. GOODBYE.

I THOUGHT THAT GUY WOULD NEVER LEAVE!

WELL, MR. RATCH IS ONE OF DADDY'S IMPORTANT BUSINESS ASSOCIATES.

THE NIGHT MARCHERS

JINKIES, WHEN I SIGNED UP FOR THE *CONFERENCE ON POLYNESIAN PARANORMAL PHENOMENA*, I NEVER THOUGHT I'D BE STAYING IN A PLACE LIKE THIS!

MR. RATCH WANTS DADDY TO BUY A CONDO HERE. SO, HE OFFERED US A SAMPLE OF WHAT HAWAIIAN CONDO LIFE IS LIKE!

SPEAKING OF SAMPLES, I CAN'T WAIT TO SAMPLE THE *LOCAL CUISINE!*

THE CONFERENCE IS SPONSORING A *WELCOMING LUAU* TONIGHT!

RUAU?

MICHAEL KRAIGER-WRITER
SCOTT NEELY-ARTIST
ROB LEIGH-LETTERER
PAUL BECTON-COLORIST
SNO-CONE-SEPARATIONS
HARVEY RICHARDS-ASST EDITOR
JOAN HILTY EDITOR

LIKE, WHERE IS EVERYBODY?

GOOD MORNING, SLEEPYHEADS! VELMA WENT TO THE CONFERENCE, AND FRED JUST HEADED TO THE BEACH WITH HIS SURFBOARD!

AND *I'M* OFF TO DO SOME HIKING! SEE YA!

LOOKS LIKE IT'S JUST YOU AND ME, SCOOB! WHAT DO YOU WANNA DO?

...ACCORDING TO *LOCAL LEGEND...*

PROGRAM

HMM?

STORY CONTINUES ON PAGE 54

MUMMY on the loose!

Help the gang to solve this mystery before that mad mummy causes chaos!

While at the Museum of Archaeology, Scooby and friends are chased by a ghastly mummy. The monster wants an ancient coin that's the key to unlocking a priceless treasure. The gang needs your help to find the coin before the mummy does.

Help unravel the mystery by finding the gold coin and these other characters that have become "wrapped up" in this mummy mystery!

Gummy Mummy

Mummy Scooby

Mr. Volt

Dr. Dig

Chef Mummy Mia

Ghostly Gardener

Gold Coin

...AND AFTER WE TRIED THE *COCONUT-MANGO* COMBINATION WE JUST HAD TO TRY THE *PAPAYA-KIWI* COMBINATION! DIDN'T WE, SCOOB?

REAH, RARAYA!

WELL, *I* LEARNED SOME VERY INTERESTING THINGS ABOUT THOSE GHOSTS YOU SAW LAST NIGHT!

ACCORDING TO PROFESSOR MOLOKI, WHAT YOU DESCRIBED SEEING WERE THE *NIGHT MARCHERS*. THEY APPEAR ON THE "NIGHT OF *KANE*"--BETWEEN THE 27TH AND 29TH OF THE MONTH OF A NEW MOON!

THE NIGHT MARCHERS ARE A PROCESSION OF GHOSTS TRAVELING TO THE OLD TEMPLES, OR HEALING STONES, KNOWN AS *HEIAU.*

IT'S SAID IF THEY CATCH A WHIFF OF A *HUMAN OBSERVER,* THAT PERSON IS DOOMED!

EEEK! LIKE, I GUESS WE MUST HAVE BEEN DOWNWIND, SCOOB!

HMMM...SOME OF THE LOCALS TOLD ME A SIMILAR STORY AT THE BEACH TODAY!

THE WEIRD THING IS, THEY USUALLY AREN'T SEEN BY *HAOLE.* THAT'S HAWAIIAN FOR CAUCASIANS.

THAT'S NOT THE *ONLY* WEIRD THING! I FOUND SOMETHING IN THE FOREST NEAR WHERE YOU SAW THE GHOSTS...

OIA!

EEE-YA!

I'VE GOT AN IDEA! I'LL USE THE FLASHLIGHT TO QUICKLY *BLIND* THEM SO WE CAN GET AWAY!

RIKES!

OK, GUYS, GET READY...

RUH?

LOOK OUT!

I GOT HIM!

AAHHH!!!

IT'S...*PROFESSOR MOLOKI*?!

PROFESSOR, WHAT ARE *YOU* DOING HERE?

AND WHO ARE ALL THESE PEOPLE?

OH, IT'S A LONG STORY...

THESE ARE MY STUDENTS FROM THE COLLEGE, AND WE WERE TRYING TO SCARE PEOPLE AWAY FROM THIS FOREST. YOU SEE, THERE IS AN **ANCIENT TEMPLE** NEARBY.

SO YOU USED GLOW STICKS AND DRY ICE TO MAKE YOURSELVES LOOK LIKE GHOSTS!

BUT WHY WERE YOU USING THE LEGEND TO SCARE PEOPLE OFF?

THE FOREST AROUND THE TEMPLE IS SCHEDULED FOR DEVELOPMENT. THEY PLAN ON TURNING IT INTO **CONDOS.**

BUT THE ANCIENT TEMPLE WAS ON MY HIKING MAP. IT'S PROTECTED BY THE STATE AND OPEN TO THE PUBLIC!

YOU DON'T UNDERSTAND. IF THEY BUILD THE CONDOS AND CHANGE THE LOOK OF THE LAND, OUR **ANCESTORS** MIGHT NOT BE ABLE TO FIND THEIR WAY TO THE TEMPLE!

WHAT DO WE DO, GANG?

WELL, THEY'RE NOT REALLY BREAKING ANY LAWS...

...AND REMEMBER WHO IT IS THAT'S PLANNING TO BUILD CONDOS HERE.

I THINK WE MAY BE ABLE TO HELP YOU!

LATER THAT NIGHT...

WHEN WE HEARD THE DRUMMING START, I CALLED YOU RIGHT AWAY!

IF THIS IS A *NOISE* COMPLAINT...

OH, BE QUIET, DEAR. WE'RE ABOUT TO EXPERIENCE THE *SUPERNATURAL!*

OH, GOOD, YOU INVITED PROFESSOR MOLOKI!

HARUMPH! THAT QUACK! HE'S BEEN HARASSING ME NOT TO BUILD MY CONDOS HERE!

WITH GOOD REASON, SIR--THIS FOREST IS HAUNTED BY THE NIGHT MARCHERS! *LOOK!*

≥sniff≤...PUT THAT *CIGAR* OUT, YOU FOOL! IF THEY SMELL IT, WE'RE *FINISHED!*

HUH?

PUM PUM PUM PUMM

ROO RATE!

OIA! OIA!

W-WHAT ARE THEY SAYING?

DON'T ASK! JUST *RUN!*

THAT WAS *THRILLING!*

THEY HAUNT THE FOREST EVERY NEW MOON, SEARCHING FOR THEIR TEMPLE.

I CAN'T BUILD LUXURY CONDOS IN A *HAUNTED FOREST!* NOBODY WILL WANT TO LIVE THERE!

WHY, I COULD HAVE LOST *MILLIONS* IF I'D BUILT CONDOS THERE. IF IT WASN'T FOR YOU KIDS AND THAT DOG...

ROOBY ROOBY ROO!

THE END

SCOOBY-DOO SEARCH!

Use your detective skills to spot all of the words hidden in the grid below.

GHOST MYSTERY
TOMB COOLSVILLE
COBWEB DAPHNE ALIEN

There is one member of the gang who isn't hiding in the grid. Can you work out which one it is?

C	O	B	W	E	B	C	L	U	E	W
T	N	I	R	P	R	E	G	N	I	F
S	T	M	G	D	H	C	T	I	W	T
C	A	Y	O	H	P	O	N	J	E	O
O	L	S	V	N	O	H	O	S	D	M
O	I	T	E	A	S	S	B	T	A	B
B	E	E	L	C	B	T	T	C	P	D
Y	N	R	M	K	B	C	E	S	H	E
S	T	Y	A	P	B	C	L	R	N	R
C	O	O	L	S	V	I	L	L	E	F

SCOOBY WITCH FINGERPRINT SHAGGY FRED
CLUE MONSTER VELMA BAT

60